Encouragement to Penitent Sinners and Joy Over Their Conversion

Encouragement
to
Penitent Sinners
and
Joy Over Their Conversion

By

John M. Brenneman

Repent and turn yourselves from all your transgressions;
so iniquity shall not be your ruin.

Ezek. 18:30

ISBN 978-1-68001-009-1

For additional titles and other material by the same author, contact:

Sermon on the Mount Publishing
P.O. Box 246
Manchester, MI 48158
(734) 428 – 0488
the-witness@sbcglobal.net
www.kingdomreading.com

Our Mission
To obey the commands of Christ and to teach men to do so.

First Printing – January 2017 – 750 copies

Present Publisher's Preface

John M. Brenneman (1816–1895) was an (Old) Mennonite bishop in Allen County, Ohio. He was a frequent writer in the *Herald of Truth*. *Encouragement to Penitent Sinners* was originally published in 1877 by John Funk's Mennonite Publishing Company in Elkhart, Indiana.

To our knowledge, this is the first printing of this booklet since Brenneman's day. We have corrected some minor spelling and grammatical mistakes, but have not attempted to bring all of Brenneman's punctuation into conformity with current standards. All subheadings and all footnotes giving verse citations were added by the current publisher. A few of Brenneman's paragraphs were split by our subheadings. All illustrations are original.

May the Lord be glorified with this booklet, and may repentant sinners be encouraged to seek the Lord while He may be found.

~Andrew V. Ste. Marie

Original Preface

There can be nothing more needful, and nothing concerning which a sinner should feel more deeply interested, than a true conversion to God, because upon it depends his eternal well-being. Therefore, it is highly necessary that a sinner under conviction should have a correct view and clear understanding of true conversion, for without a true knowledge on this most important subject, he might easily be led astray by accepting that for conversion which is a mere deception.

The author of the following treatise has aimed to set forth the true idea of Gospel conversion in as clear a light and comprehensive a manner as he was able, and it is hoped that no truly convicted sinner will, after reading it, have reason to complain and say it is too dark, mysterious and unintelligible to benefit anyone. And as we are so plainly taught in the Holy Bible that the sinner must repent and be truly converted to God in order to become happy in eternity, the Author earnestly begs the reader that he would attentively and seriously examine the following discourse, in which he has tried to aid, encourage, and animate humbled and penitent sinners in the good work, and to point them to Jesus, the Author of Salvation. And notwithstanding the wretched and most deplorable state and condition of a sinner, while in a state of nature, the reader will find in the following explanations how such a one may, by true, heartfelt repentance and by true faith in Jesus Christ, become converted and translated into a state of grace, peace, and newness of life, and by such a change may create a joy in heaven, in the presence of the angels of God, which is truly encouraging to mourning, penitent sinners.

Further, it is also maintained that a person must be either converted or unconverted, righteous or unrighteous, holy or unholy, yea, that he must be either a child of God or a child of the wicked one, and that there is no middle way, but that a person must be either walking on the broad, or on the narrow way; and that he is either gathering with Christ, or scattering abroad, and can positively not serve Christ and Belial at the same time. Hence we may plainly see, that it is far from being sufficient to have merely "a name that we live, while we are dead." The sinner must really undergo a change, and be thoroughly converted. He must be born of God, must become a new creature, that is, he must pass from death unto life, from darkness to light, and from the power of Satan to God; and thus must walk in newness of life, and "Live soberly, righteously, and godly in this present world," in order to become happy in heaven. And where such a change has indeed been wrought in man, he will doubtless also experience, and know more or less of it; for such a godly and new life is not obtained while sleeping.

The above is the doctrinal standpoint from which this little work has been written. May God add his blessing thereto, that it may be the means of bringing sinners to repentance, that God may be glorified and angels rejoice as intimated in the text, and the author shall feel himself richly rewarded.

~J.M.B.

The prodigal's return. Luke 15:20

An Encouragement to Penitent Sinners, and Joy Over Their Conversion

I say unto you, that likewise joy shall be in heaven over one sinner that repenteth, more than over ninety and nine just persons, which need no repentance.
Luke 15:7

When once the deeply fallen sinner becomes truly convicted and wakes up from the sleep of sin, and by the Spirit of God is brought to a true self-knowledge, is made to see and feel his wretched and most deplorable condition, and that he becomes aware what a poor, lost sinner he is, and that his sins now as a burden, become too heavy for him to bear, that he in sorrow and penitence feels truly contrite and cast down, he would, in such misery and sore distress, have to sink into utter despair if it were not for the consoling and encouraging promises and kind invitations of God in his word to awakened sinners, such as the following:

"Though your sins be as scarlet, they shall be as white as snow; though they be red like crimson, they shall be as wool." Isa. 1:18. "For thus saith the high and lofty One that inhabiteth eternity, whose name is holy; I dwell in the high and holy place, with him also that is of a contrite and humble spirit, to revive the spirit of the humble, and to revive the heart of the contrite ones." 57:15. "To this man will I look, even to him that is poor, and of a contrite spirit, and trembleth at my word." 66:2. "Look unto me and be ye saved, all ye ends of the earth." 45:22. "The Lord is nigh unto them that are of a broken heart; and saveth such as be of a contrite spirit." Psa. 34:18. "As I live saith the Lord God, I have no pleasure in the death of the wicked; but that the wicked turn from his way and live: turn ye, turn ye from your evil ways; for why will ye die?" Ezek. 33:11. "Where sin abounded, grace did much more abound." Rom. 5:20. "Draw nigh to God, and he will draw nigh to you." James 4:8. "God will have all men to be saved and to come unto the knowledge of the truth." 1 Tim. 2:4. "This is a faithful saying, and worthy of all acceptation, that Christ Jesus came into the world, to save sinners." 1 Tim. 1:15. The Lord "is long suffering to usward, not willing that any should perish, but that all should come to repentance." 2 Pet. 3:9. "Believe on the Lord Jesus Christ, and thou shalt be saved." Acts 16:31. "He that believeth on him shall not be confounded." 1 Pet. 2:6. But especially consoling and encouraging for the penitent sinner are the words of our text: "I say unto you, that likewise joy shall be in heaven over one sinner that repenteth, more than over ninety and nine just persons, which need no repentance."

That God is willing that all truly penitent souls should be saved may be easily known by this, that he sent his beloved Son into the world for the express purpose of saving them. "For God so loved the world, that he gave his only begotten Son, that whosoever believeth in him should not perish, but have everlasting life; for God sent not his Son into the world to condemn the world; but that the world through him might be saved." "He that spared not his own Son, but delivered him up for us all, how shall he not with him also freely give us all things." In the Son of God was the prophetical Scripture fulfilled. "The Spirit of the Lord is upon me, because he hath anointed me to preach the Gospel to the poor; he hath sent me to heal the brokenhearted, to preach deliverance to the captives, and recovering of sight to the blind; to set at liberty them that are bruised, to preach the acceptable year of the Lord." Luke 4:18, 19.

Jesus is merciful

Jesus wrought many signs and wonders among the people, he "went about doing good, and healing all that were oppressed of the devil." He made the blind to see, the lame to walk, cleansed the lepers, made the deaf to hear, and raised the dead. He preached the glad tidings of eternal salvation and of the kingdom of God so convincingly that "the people were astonished at his doctrine, for he taught them as one having authority, and not as the Scribes." So affecting and penetrating was his teaching, that many were touched thereby, and caused to reflect; even his enemies acknowledged that "never man spake like this man." He invited all who "labored and were heavy laden, to come unto him, and he would give them rest;" "and him that cometh to me," said he, "I will in no wise cast out."

So kind, so merciful, and benevolent was Jesus, that all the people were very attentive to hear him; and in him was the prophecy of Jacob fulfilled: "And unto him shall the gathering of the people be." Gen. 49:10. And in the beginning of the chapter from which our text is taken, we find that "then drew near unto him all the publicans and sinners for to hear him, and the Pharisees and scribes murmured, saying: This man receiveth sinners, and eateth with them."

Jesus rebukes hypocrisy

The Pharisees were a very strict sect in their outward worship, and also did many good works, merely to be seen and heard of men, to gain their applause. But Jesus, who well knew what was in their hearts, frequently rebuked them for their hypocrisy: "Outwardly," said he, "ye appear righteous unto men, but within ye are full of hypocrisy and iniquity." For that reason, they were his enemies and hated him, and sought whenever there was an opportunity, to make him odious before the people. Therefore they accused him that he received sinners and ate with them, as if he had been a very bad man, because he made company with such sinful men. But thereby they gave to him, though unconsciously, a most glorious testimony of his kindness. We have great reason to thank God, that Jesus receives sinners, and that he was sent out of love into the world to seek and to save them; if such was not the case, we would all be lost.

Mercy to sinners

The publicans were those who received or collected the tribute—toll—or tax; and it is likely that there were also bad men among them, who sometimes deceived the people by collecting too much of them. Therefore did John the Baptist warn them, to "exact no more, than that which was appointed them." Luke 3:13.

Zacchaeus, who was chief among the publicans, said to Jesus, (who had called him to ". . . make haste and come down from

the tree"), "Behold, Lord the half of my goods I give to the poor; and if I have taken anything from any man by false accusation, I restore him fourfold." He joyfully received Jesus into his house. Such publicans Jesus gladly accepted; or such as the publican who went into the temple to pray, and "smote upon his breast, saying, 'God be merciful to me a sinner.'" (Reader, did you ever thus confess your sins to God and pray for mercy, with a sincere and contrite heart?) Or such as the publican named Levi, who was sitting "at the receipt of custom" (collecting custom money), at the bidding of Jesus, "left all, and followed him;" or such as the woman called a sinner, who wept and washed the feet of Jesus with tears, and did wipe them with the hairs of her head, kissed and anointed them (behold, what an example of repentance, love, and humility); her he also did not send away comfortless, but said unto her, "Thy sins are forgiven," and bade her "go in peace." Such penitent sinners did Jesus receive, and doth still receive, and eateth, and holdeth spiritual communion with them.

Joy over finding that which was lost

Jesus well knew how to defend himself before the scribes and Pharisees, by setting forth beautiful and well-adapted parables. "And he spake this parable unto them, saying, What man of you having (owning) a hundred sheep, if he lose one of them, doth not leave the ninety and nine in the wilderness, and go after that which is lost until he find it." So valuable was a single sheep then estimated, although the man had yet ninety and nine (a goodly number) left as his own, he yet considered it worth the toil, perhaps out of compassion, to go after the one strayed sheep, seeking it until he had found it. "And when he hath found it, he layeth it on his shoulders rejoicing." Was it so weary that it could not walk any more? He took it in mercy on his shoulders and carried it home. (A beautiful representation of the mercy and kindness of Jesus, to penitent sinners.) "And when he cometh home, he calleth together his friends and neighbors, saying unto them, Rejoice with me; for I have found my sheep which was lost."[1] If ye then so anxiously take pains, in seeking one single strayed sheep (Jesus means to say), and thus rejoice when ye have found it, why then do you blame me for seeking, and by grace accepting, poor, strayed and lost mankind, who are so much better than a sheep? For therefore did he indeed come, to seek "the lost sheep of the house of Israel,"[2] and to save them, as he also had promised, saying: "I, even I, will both search my sheep, and seek them out." Ezek. 34:11. And again it is said: "He shall feed his flock like a shepherd; . . . he shall gather the lambs with his arms, and carry

1 Luke 15:3-6.
2 Matthew 15:24.

them in his bosom."[3] So full of compassion is Jesus, to poor lost sinners, and so gladly does he receive them, if they repent. "I say unto you," said Jesus, "that likewise joy shall be in heaven over one sinner that repenteth, more than over ninety and nine just persons, which need no repentance."[4] Oh how consoling and encouraging are these words for a sorely distressed, and truly penitent and mourning sinner! "I say unto you, that likewise joy shall be in heaven, over one sinner that repenteth." Do then give ear, poor, troubled sinner: wilt thou not also create a joy in heaven by your repentance? Which if it is sincere, must be of great value, otherwise it could not cause a joy in heaven. Yea, doubtless, your everlasting joy and well-being is depending upon it. Oh then, neglect it not, but do sincerely repent while you may.

Repentance unto conversion

The word *repentance* in our text signifies more than merely acknowledging our sins with our mouths before men; it means a deep, heartfelt sorrow for sin, which will cause the sinner to "go mourning all the day long,"[5] for where true repentance exists, the sinner will most painfully feel the burden of his sins, will feel deeply stricken and bowed down because of them, and is brought into such a penitent and mourning condition as will cause him now to forsake and sincerely hate sin, and earnestly to pray for forgiveness of the same; and by the influence and power of God's Spirit and true faith in Jesus, he now turns, or becomes converted, from darkness to light, and from the power of Satan unto God, and through his Holy Spirit becomes changed and renewed; yea, is born again, and thus is translated into a spiritual, godly and heavenly state and life, that he from henceforth will walk in newness of life. For a true, evangelical, heartfelt repentance, which alone is pleasing to God, and a true conversion, belong together, and are so closely connected, that it is impossible to separate them, because where true repentance exists, or has taken place, there is also a true conversion to God.

---

3 Isaiah 40:11.
4 Luke 15:7.
5 Psalm 38:6.

In the Dutch (Holland) our text reads as follows: "Thus shall be joy in heaven over one sinner that converteth himself, more than over ninety and nine righteous ones, which have no need of conversion." The latter clause of this passage is doubtless to be understood of those who need not that total change or conversion, which is requisite at the beginning of the Christian course, where a person passeth from death unto life, and from the broad road into the narrow way.

This rendering is not at all opposed to the English translation, because we know that true repentance and conversion are closely connected, and where one in truth exists, the other must also be. Peter said: "Repent ye therefore and be converted, that your sins may be blotted out."[6] Both are necessary to having our sins blotted out.

Conversion = turning around

The word *turn*, or *return*, is frequently used in the Bible to signify conversion, and I wish in particular to have it so understood in this discourse, where it is used. It is often so rendered in the German, which is also correct, because true conversion in reality, is a turning, from darkness to light—from the power of Satan unto God, and from sin to holiness. Repent, and turn yourselves[7] from all your transgressions; so iniquity shall not be your ruin." Ezek. 18:30. "Turn ye, turn ye, from your evil ways." 33:11. "Therefore also now saith the Lord, Turn ye even to me with all your heart, and with fasting, and with weeping, and with mourning; and rend your heart, and not your garments, and turn unto the Lord your God; for he is gracious, merciful, slow to anger, and of great kindness." Joel 2:12, 13.

It is true, in this earnest call to turn, nothing is said of repentance, but where fasting, weeping, mourning, and heart-rending take place, there doubtless repentance is also included. Paul "shewed unto them of Damascus, and at Jerusalem, and throughout all the coasts of Judea, and then to the Gentiles, that they should

---

6 Acts 3:19.

7 Convert yourselves, German.—*Author's footnote.*

repent and turn to God, and do works meet for repentance."[8] Here repentance and turning (that is, conversion), are joined together.

Nineveh turned around

Jesus testified of the Ninevites that they repented at the teaching of Jonah. Now we find that when Jonah began to enter into the city of Nineveh a day's journey, "he cried and said: Yet forty days, and Nineveh shall be overthrown, so the people of Nineveh believed God, and proclaimed a fast, and put on sackcloth."[9] "The king himself arose from his throne and laid his robe from him, and covered himself with sackcloth, and sat in ashes, and caused it to be proclaimed," . . . that "neither man nor beast," . . . should "taste anything," . . . and that they should "cry mightily unto God, yea, let them turn every one from his evil way, and from the violence that is in their hands."[10] And when "God saw their works, that they turned from their evil way," he "repented of the evil, that he had said that he would do unto them; and he did it not."[11] Here it is said, "that they turned." The Savior says, "they repented."[12]

Thus turning and repenting were connected. And although we do not always find these sentences together, the one is nevertheless generally included in the other. As for instance: God "now commandeth all men everywhere to repent, because he hath appointed a day, in the which he will judge the world."[13] And again, "The Lord is longsuffering to us-ward, not willing that any should perish, but that all should come to repentance."[14] In neither of these passages is conversion mentioned, but is evidently included in both. Jesus' first instruction was: "The time is fulfilled, and the kingdom of God is at hand; repent ye and believe the Gospel."[15] It was also one of his last commands, that "repentance and remission of sins should be preached, in his name among all nations."[16]

---

8 Acts 26:20.
9 Jonah 3:4-5.
10 Jonah 3:6-8.
11 Jonah 3:10.
12 Matthew 12:41.
13 Acts 17:30-31.
14 II Peter 3:9.
15 Mark 1:15.
16 Luke 24:47.

This command, the apostles were also diligent to fulfill. When on the day of Pentecost the word preached entered into the hearts of the people, and they said, "Men and brethren, what shall we do? Then Peter said unto them, Repent and be baptized every one of you, in the name of Jesus Christ for the remission of sins, and ye shall receive the gift of the Holy Ghost,"[17] which is still a proper advice to sinners under conviction. Paul "testified both to the Jews, and also to the Greeks, repentance toward God, and faith toward our Lord Jesus Christ."[18] In none of these passages is conversion mentioned, yet we know that without conversion, repentance would have been of no value.

Repentance + conversion = new life

We also read "of the conversion of the Gentiles." Acts 15:3. "My sentence is, that we trouble not them, which from among the Gentiles are turned to God." Verse 19. "And a great number believed, and turned unto the Lord." Chap. 11:21. "And preach unto you, that ye should turn from these vanities, unto the living God." Chap. 14:15. And again, "Ye turned to God from idols." 1 Thess. 1:9. In these passages there is nothing said of repentance, but we also know, that without repentance, there could be no true turning, or conversion to God. Paul[19] said unto the Jews: "Unto you first, God having raised up his Son Jesus, sent him to bless you, in turning away every one of you from his iniquities." Acts 3:26. Again, "Him hath God exalted with his right hand, to be a Prince and a Savior, for to give repentance to Israel, and forgiveness of sins." Acts 5:31. Thus, then, was Jesus raised up and sent to the Jews, to bless them and turn them, and was also exalted to be a Prince, to give unto them repentance, that is, to call, and have them called, to repentance. And where sincere repentance, and turning to God with earnest prayer take place, or be joined together, there will also, without doubt, a new life commence, because there a person is born again of God, and of his Spirit, and becomes a child of God. There is also true faith, out of which obedience will follow. Such persons will willingly take the yoke of Christ upon them,

17 Acts 2:38.
18 Acts 20:21.
19 *Sic* – Peter.

and keep his commandments and precepts; they will also "as new born babes, desire the sincere milk of the word, that they may grow thereby."[20] They will "let their lights shine before men, that they may see their good works."[21] With them, old things "have passed away, and all things have become new."[22] Among them will be brotherly "love without dissimulation."[23] They "are risen with Christ," and "seek those things which are above."[24] They "are led by the Spirit of God, and walk after the Spirit,"[25] which "will guide them into all truth."[26] They will also deny ungodliness and worldly lusts, and "live soberly, righteously and godly in this present world."[27] Reader, has such a new life ever been wrought in you? If not, oh give yourself no rest, until you obtain it.

The prodigal returns to his father

We have also a clear representation of true repentance and conversion set forth in the parable of the prodigal son, in the chapter of which our text is a part. When he had wasted all his substance, and found himself in great need, and unable to sustain himself any more, "he came to himself," that is, to a self-knowledge, he said: "How many hired servants of my father have bread enough and to spare, and I perish with hunger. I will arise and go to my father, and will say unto him, Father, I have sinned against heaven and before thee."[28] He also carried out his resolution: he arose, and came to his father, and when he was yet a great way off, his father saw him, and had compassion, and ran, and fell on his neck, and kissed him. And the son said unto him, "Father, I have sinned against heaven and in thy sight, and am no more worthy to be called thy son."[29] (Such a feeling and confession doth still accompany true repentance.) But the father said to his servants, "Bring

20 I Peter 2:2.
21 Matthew 5:16.
22 II Corinthians 5:17.
23 Romans 12:9.
24 Colossians 3:1.
25 Romans 8:1, 4, 14.
26 John 16:13.
27 Titus 2:12.
28 Luke 15:17-18.
29 Luke 15:21.

hither the best robe and put it on him," which may signify the robe of righteousness. "And put a ring on his hand," which may signify that confidential trust and love which will now exist between God and a true convert. "And shoes on his feet,"[30] which may perhaps signify having our "feet shod (spiritually) with the preparation of the Gospel of peace," (Eph. 6:15) to enable us to walk on the narrow path, and to tread "on serpents and scorpions, and over all the power of the enemy," without being hurt. Luke 10:19. "And bring hither the fatted calf, and kill it, and let us eat and be merry, for this my son was dead and is alive again (mark); he was lost, and is found. And they began to be merry."[31] Thus "likewise joy shall be in heaven," our text says, "over one sinner that repenteth." Though but one, how much more when a goodly number repent.

Turn and live!

The prodigal son was not reproached on account of his great sins; he confessed them and received forgiveness. "He that confesseth and forsaketh his sins, shall have mercy." Prov. 28:13. Thus, if the wicked "turn" from his wickedness, "none of his sins that he hath committed, shall be mentioned unto him." Ezek. 33:16. Poor, troubled, penitent, sinsick sinner, take courage. "Draw nigh to God (in fervent prayer), and he will draw nigh unto you."[32] "Turn and live."[33] Thus the penitent, converted sinner, obtains peace with God, and the spirit of adoption, through which he can, with a filial confidence, "cry, Abba, Father." To such a one, "the Spirit itself beareth witness, that he is a child of God." Rom. 8:16. Such a conversion and reconciliation of a sinner to God causeth joy in heaven, "in the presence of the angels of God," (verse 10) who are ministering spirits, sent forth to minister for them, who shall be heirs of salvation." Heb. 1:14. They are said to be "innumerable." When Jesus was apprehended by his enemies, he might have prayed to his heavenly Father, who should presently have given him "more than twelve legions of angels,"[34]

30 Luke 15:22.
31 Luke 15:23-24.
32 James 4:8a.
33 cf. Ezekiel 18:32.
34 Matthew 26:53.

to rescue him. A legion is said to be about six thousand. Twelve legions therefore would be seventy-two thousand. Now if one angel could smite, in one night, in the camp of the Assyrians, one hundred fourscore and five thousand men (2 Kings 19:35), what think ye could twelve legions do? They are frequently called "mighty angels." One angel preserved the three Hebrews in the fiery furnace unhurt, and also Daniel in the lion's den, and rescued Peter out of prison. Thus "The angel of the Lord encampeth round about them that fear him, and delivereth them."[35]

Joy over sinners turned around

It seems that our conditions here upon earth are well known unto the angels; they know whether we fear God or not. These mighty angels seem to be deeply interested in the salvation of sinners, and why then should sinners themselves be careless of it? The birth of Christ was made known to the shepherds by an angel. "Behold," said he, "I bring you good tidings of great joy, which shall be to all people, for unto you is born this day in the city of David, a Savior, which is Christ the Lord."[36] "And suddenly there was with the angel a multitude of the heavenly host, praising God, and saying, Glory to God in the highest, on earth peace, good will toward men."[37] Thus, it seems, the angels rejoiced at the birth of the Savior, who had come to call sinners to repentance, and to save them; and it is therefore no wonder that they also rejoice over penitent and converted sinners, because they doubtless well know that the converted children of God shall, in the resurrection, "be equal" unto themselves. Luke 20:36. But not only the angels, but doubtless also all truly converted persons will rejoice over penitent, converted sinners; yea the converted themselves will rejoice over their own conversion. The jailer "rejoiced believing in God with all his house."[38] And the eunuch after he was baptized "went on his way rejoicing."[39] And oh, how shall we rejoice with the holy angels, if we may ever be so fortunate as to get to where they

35 Psalm 34:7.
36 Luke 2:11.
37 Luke 2:13-14.
38 Acts 16:34.
39 Acts 8:39.

are, in the presence of God, where is "fullness of joy, at his right hand, and pleasures for evermore."[40] Although we here "sow in tears," we shall there "reap in joy."[41] Yea we shall "rejoice with joy unspeakable and full of glory."[42]

Who are the 99 righteous ones?

But who are the ninety and nine just persons, which need no repentance? On this expositors differ in their views. The reading, both of the German, and Dutch (Holland), is "righteous ones." But these different terms have precisely the same meaning, because he who is truly righteous, is also just, and the just, righteous as we shall yet see. Some assert that by the ninety and nine just, or righteous persons, which need no repentance, the Savior refers to the angels in heaven. Others again say that he has reference to little children. And a third class maintain that the self-righteous are meant, such as the scribes and Pharisees, and many of the Jews, who went "about to establish their own righteousness." Rom. 10:3. And yet a fourth class maintain, that the truly converted, justified children of God, called the sheep and flock of Christ, are referred to in the text. That the first three assertions are incorrect, and the fourth one correct, is the honest belief of the writer.

Jesus said Luke 5:32: "I came not to call the righteous, but sinners to repentance." Now there is not the least doubt in my mind that these righteous, and the righteous referred to in our text, are the same kind or class of persons; therefore they cannot be angels, but must be men here on earth, because it would not have made good sense, for the Savior to have said, I came not to call angels to repentance, because their residence is in heaven. That the Savior did not refer to little children, seems quite clear also, because the word righteous is nowhere applied to them in the Bible, to my recollection. The Lord was willing to spare Sodom for the sake of ten righteous persons, but that number could no more be found there; but who would assert, that ten little children could not have been found there? That the ninety and nine righteous or just persons, which need no repentance, are not the self-righteous,

40 Psalm 16:11.

41 Psalm 126:5.

42 I Peter 1:8.

to whom Jesus referred, seems to me very plain, because none stand in greater need of repentance than they. The self-righteous scribes and Pharisees belonged to the lost sheep of the house of Israel, to whom Jesus was especially sent, and how often would he have gathered them under the wings of his mercy, and they "would not?" His first teaching to them was, "Repent and believe the Gospel."[43] And before his ascension to heaven, he commanded that "repentance and remission of sins should be preached in his name among all nations;"[44] consequently also to the self-righteous. If in our text, Jesus had reference to the self-righteous, then the joy in heaven over the conversion of sinners is not near so great as I believe it is.

When it is said that there is *more* joy over one sinner that repenteth than over ninety-nine just persons, which need no repentance, it is evidently implied that there is also some joy over the ninety and nine. The word "more" does not include all the joy. But who would maintain that the angels in heaven could in the least degree rejoice over ninety and nine self-righteous persons? Much more would they have reason to mourn over them, because the self-righteous are in a very dangerous condition; they fancy themselves to be "rich and increased with goods, and to have need of nothing, and know not that they are wretched, and miserable, and poor, and blind, and naked."[45] I wonder that ministers of the Gospel ever conceived such a thought, that the ninety and nine signify the self-righteous, because it is the duty of ministers to make dark things plain, and not plain things dark.

Now if it can be fully substantiated by the word of God, that the fourth view is correct, then that will sufficiently prove the first three incorrect. The fourth assertion is, that the ninety-nine righteous or just persons, which need no repentance (need not that converting repentance, that total change, or reformation), are regenerated, justified, believing children of God, who have "passed from death unto life,"[46] "and from the power of Satan unto God,"[47]

43 Mark 1:15.
44 Luke 24:47.
45 Revelation 3:17.
46 John 5:24; I John 3:14.
47 Acts 26:18.

and "walk in newness of life,"[48] and "are in Christ Jesus," so that "there is now no more condemnation against them." Rom. 8:1.

And you?

Dear reader, have you experienced such a change? Examine yourself honestly, as nothing can be more needful than a true conversion to God in order to be happy in eternity. "For ye must be born again."[49] Peter in writing to the believers, says, "Ye were as sheep going astray; but are now returned (converted, German) unto the Shepherd and Bishop of your souls."[50] Evidently, they were now no more strayed sheep. Jesus says, "I am the good Shepherd, and know my sheep, and am known of mine."[51] And again, "*My sheep hear my voice, and I know them, and they follow me.*"[52] Jesus' sheep then are converted, justified, and newborn souls, who "*hear his voice, and follow him*" on the narrow way. And these are they who in the Scriptures, are expressly called, "the righteous," "the just," because they "are justified, in the name of the Lord Jesus, and by the Spirit of our God." 1 Cor. 6:11. When men are justified, they are pardoned, and made free from the bondage of sin (Rom. 6:18), and are received into the favor of God as righteous.

Why are "none righteous"?

But here someone might answer with the quotation of Paul, Rom. 3:10, "There is none righteous, no, not one." But these words cannot at all, with propriety, be applied unto the converted children of God, but only to the unconverted children of this world, who yet live in their old state of nature. The apostle had just mentioned in verse 9 that "both Jews and Gentiles" "were all under sin, as it is written, There is none righteous, no not one." This passage in verse ten, as also the eight following verses, the apostle quoted from the Old Testament, and these nine verses stand in close connection or belong together, so that he who would

48 Romans 6:4.
49 John 3:7.
50 I Peter 2:25.
51 John 10:14.
52 John 10:27.

appeal to Rom. 3:10, "there is none righteous," etc., to prove the unrighteousness of all men, converted as well as unconverted, and is yet willing to have these words applied unto himself, must also, upon the same ground, be willing to have the eight following verses applied unto himself; because Paul applies them all unto the same unrighteous characters. They read as follows: "There is none that understandeth, there is none that seeketh after God, they are all gone out of the way, they are together become unprofitable; there is none that doeth good, no, not one, their throat is an open sepulcher; with their tongues they have used deceit; the poison of asps is under their lips: whose mouth is full of cursing and bitterness: their feet are swift to shed blood: destruction and misery are in their ways; and the way of peace have they not known. There is no fear of God before their eyes."

Justified = made righteous

I hope that no enlightened man will maintain that the above-described wickedness may yet be committed or practiced by a converted child of God. I doubt not in the least that he who is yet guilty of such vices and transgressions is a wicked and unrighteous person, and "the *unrighteous shall not inherit the kingdom of God*."[53] Therefore, they must be made righteous, that is, must be justified. Now after the conclusion of the above description of the wicked, the apostle says, "Now we know that what things soever the law saith, it saith to them who are under the law; that every mouth may be stopped, and all the world may become guilty before God"[54] (all boasting be excluded). Therefore, the above description of transgressors, can by no means be applied to the converted, because they "are not under the law, but under grace." "For sin shall not have dominion over you: for ye are not under the law, but under grace. What then? Shall we sin, because we are not under the law, but under grace? God forbid." Rom. 6:14, 15. And again, "If ye be led by the Spirit, ye are not under the law." Gal. 5:18. "They that are led by the Spirit of God, they are the sons of God."[55] It was doubtless the design of Paul in this chapter

53 I Corinthians 6:9.
54 Romans 3:19.
55 Romans 8:14.

(Rom. 3), to show that all men were sinners by nature, and that they stand upon an equal footing before God. He says: (verses 22, 23) "For there is no difference, for all have sinned, and come short of the glory of God."

Made righteous by grace

Someone might ask, How then are they justified? The apostle tells us in the next verse: "Being justified freely by his grace,

through the redemption that is in Christ Jesus;" and verse 28: "Therefore we conclude that a man is justified by faith, without the deeds of the law." To be justified then means to receive the full pardon and forgiveness of our sins, and by faith in Christ, and through, or on account of, his atoning blood to be received into the favor of God as just or righteous. "By him (Jesus) all that believe are justified from all things, from which ye could not be justified by the law of Moses." Acts 13:39. "Therefore being justified by faith, we have peace with God through our Lord Jesus Christ." Rom. 5:1. "For Christ is the end of the law for righteousness, to every one that believeth." 10:4. "By his knowledge shall my righteous servant justify many." Isa. 53:11. (Ger. make many righteous). "For as by one man's disobedience, many were made sinners, so by the obedience of one shall many be made righteous." Rom. 5:19. "He that doeth righteousness is righteous." 1 John 3:7. "The righteous hath hope in his death." Prov. 14:32. "Say ye to the righteous, that it shall be well with him." Isa. 3:10. "The righteous shall go into life eternal." Matt. 25:46.

That the righteous are also called the just, may be seen in the following: "The path of the just is as the shining light." Prov. 4:18. "Noah was a just man and perfect." Gen. 6:9. "The Lord said unto Noah, Come thou and thy house into the ark; for thee have I found righteous before me." 7:1. Joseph, the husband of Mary "was a just man."[56] "There was a man in Jerusalem whose name was Simeon; and the same was just and devout."[57] "Herod feared John, knowing that he was a just man and holy."[58] "The just shall live by faith."[59]

If any should ask how people were justified before Christ made the atonement, I would answer that it was through faith in the promised Redeemer who was to make the atonement; like Abraham, who "believed God, and it was counted unto him for righteousness." Rom. 4:3.

It seems to me that our text contains precisely the same meaning as Matt. 18:12, 13. There the Savior asks his disciples: "How think ye? If a man have a hundred sheep, and one of them be gone astray, doth he not leave the ninety and nine, and goeth into the mountains and seeketh that which is gone astray? and if so be that he find it, verily I say unto you, he rejoiceth more of that sheep, than of the ninety and nine which went not astray."

---

56 Matthew 1:19.
57 Luke 2:25.
58 Mark 6:20.
59 Romans 1:17; Galatians 3:11; Hebrews 10:38; cf. Habakkuk 2:4.

The 99 are not the self-righteous

Now who would here undertake to maintain that the ninety-nine sheep which went not astray, signify self-righteous persons? Do but impartially, and candidly with open eyes, take a proper view of the matter. A man has a hundred sheep, they are all his own, only one of them is gone astray; do not the ninety-nine sheep which went not astray, still continue to be his sheep the same as before? Doubtless you must answer in the affirmative. Thus also has the Lord a flock upon earth, which he calls his own—"the righteous"—"the just." But if once in a while, one of them should fall as did Peter, the same will also, like Peter, have to be converted again, and do the first works, in order to be saved.

Tell me, were not each of the nine pieces of silver, which were not lost, precisely equal in value with the piece which was lost and found again? Certainly, and yet it was only for the found piece that the woman said, "Rejoice with me."[60] For instance, a father has ten children, and one of them wanders away, and is lost in a forest; the father, with his neighbors, painfully seeks, day after day, for the lost child; and if so be that they finally find it, the joy over that child will now be much greater than over the nine which were not lost; nevertheless, the nine would still be the father's dear and beloved children, even as before. And if he even had yet ninety-nine children, the joy would still be greatest over the one which was found.

God has always had a righteous people

In the very darkest ages of the world, the Lord had still a people upon the earth, greater or smaller in number; even under idolatrous Israel, he reserved him seven thousand which had not bowed the knees unto Baal. When Jesus expired upon the cross, "the graves were opened; *and many bodies of the saints* which slept, arose."[61] The righteous are called saints. One would almost be inclined to suppose that at the time of Christ's crucifixion, very few righteous persons were left upon the earth any more, and yet we find, that before he ascended to heaven, "he was seen of above

60 Luke 15:9.

61 Matthew 27:52 – this actually happened at Jesus' resurrection (see verse 53).

five hundred brethren at once."[62] These brethren doubtless, were just persons. The "great multitude" which John beheld, which no man could number, clothed with white robes, were "of all nations, and kindreds, and people, and tongues." Rev. 7:9.

God ever had, since men have existed, a people upon earth, called his own, his children, the just, "the righteous nation, which keepeth the truth." Isa. 26:2. Also "a holy nation, a peculiar people."[63] Sometimes called "his flock," "his church," "the saints," the "perfect," "the upright." Not that any person here in this life, is strictly, in the full sense of the word, really perfect: but the children of God are frequently so called, perhaps because they are upright, sincere, honest, and sound in the faith, to distinguish them from the ungodly. Doubtless God's children are daily aiming and longing to become more and more perfect, but a full state of perfection they can only obtain beyond the grave.

Job was a man that "was perfect and upright, and one that feared God, and eschewed evil."[64] "The just, upright man is laughed to scorn." Job 12:4. God said to Abraham: "Walk before me, and be thou perfect."[65] "The generation of the upright shall be blessed." Ps. 112:2. "The prayer of the upright is the Lord's delight." Prov. 15:8. "Mark the perfect man, and behold the upright, for the end of that man is peace." Ps. 37:37. Unto such a one it will finally be said: "Well done, thou good and faithful servant, thou hast been faithful over a few things, I will make thee ruler over many things, enter thou into the joy of thy Lord."[66] There is not the least doubt, but those who live upright before God, will meet a happy end; they are the righteous, with whom "it shall be well." "Verily there is a reward for the righteous."[67] "Let me die the death of the righteous, and let my last end be like his."[68] O what a blessed end that will be.

---

62 I Corinthians 15:6.
63 I Peter 2:9.
64 Job 1:1.
65 Genesis 17:1.
66 Matthew 25:21.
67 Psalm 58:11.
68 Numbers 23:10b.

True hope

Dear reader, Do you hope such to be your end? If so, upon what is your hope grounded? O be not deceived with a false hope. We find in Matthew 9:11–13, the Pharisees said unto Christ's disciples: Why eateth your master with publicans and sinners? But when Jesus heard that, he said unto them, They that be whole need not a physician, but they that are sick; but go ye and learn what that meaneth, I will have mercy and not sacrifice; for I came not to call the righteous, but sinners to repentance." The sick here signify sinners, and the whole, the righteous ones. A physician cannot cure or heal those that are whole, but the sick. Ministers of the Gospel must call sinners to repentance, and not the righteous. Abel "obtained witness that he was righteous." Heb. 11:4. Noah was righteous before God. "Rejoice, O ye righteous, for praise is comely for the upright." Ps. 33:1. "The righteous shall flourish like the palm tree." Ps. 92:12. "The righteous shall be in everlasting remembrance," 112:6. Zacharias and Elisabeth "were both righteous before God, walking in all the commandments and ordinances of the Lord blameless."[69] "The righteous shall shine forth as the sun in the kingdom of their Father."[70] "The effectual fervent prayer of a righteous man availeth much."[71]

Surely these things are not spoken of the self-righteous. For charitable deeds, men "shall be recompensed at the resurrection of the just." Luke 14:14. "The memory of the just is blessed." Prov. 10:7. "The way of the just is uprightness." Isa. 26:7. "If a man be just, and do that which is lawful and right . . . he shall surely live saith the Lord God." Ezek. 18:5, 9. Thus the people of God are denominated by these different terms, as righteous, just, upright, and good, to contradistinguish them from the wicked and the sinner, with whom they are often placed in contrast in the Bible, as may be seen in the following:

Abraham spake unto the Lord, saying: "That be far from thee to do after this manner, to slay the righteous with the wicked, and that the righteous should be as the wicked."[72] "The little that a

69 Luke 1:6.
70 Matthew 13:43a.
71 James 5:16b.
72 Genesis 18:25.

righteous man hath is better than the riches of many wicked."[73] "They that are of a froward heart, are abomination to the Lord, but such as are upright in their way, are his delight." Prov. 11:20. "The sacrifice of the wicked is abomination to the Lord, but the prayer of the upright is his delight." 15:8. God "maketh his sun to rise on the good and on the evil, and sendeth rain on the just and on the unjust."[74] Joseph of Arimathea is called a good and just man. Barnabas "was a good man, and full of the Holy Ghost."[75] "A good man, out of the good treasure of his heart, bringeth forth good things."[76] Paul taught that there was to be a resurrection both "of the just and the unjust."[77] "The Lord is far from the wicked, but he heareth the prayer of the righteous." Prov. 15:29. "Behold the righteous shall be recompensed in the earth: much more the wicked and the sinner." 11:31. "The ungodly shall not stand in the judgment, nor sinners in the congregation of the righteous, for the Lord knoweth the way of the righteous; but the way of the ungodly shall perish."[78] "We know that God heareth not sinners (while impenitent): but if any man be a worshipper of God, and doeth his will, him he heareth." John 9:31. "And if the righteous scarcely be saved, where shall the ungodly and the sinner appear?"[79]

And although the just or righteous need no more such a repentance and reformation as do the unconverted, which is necessary at the beginning of a Christian life, yet are we not at all, or by any means to understand, that the converted are now so unspotted, pure and holy that they could in no wise, commit the least fault anymore, or had any more need to pray, "forgive us our transgressions and sins;" for the reverse is but too often, and clearly manifested. The apostle James says: "In many things we offend all" (including himself). "If any man offend not in word, the same is a perfect man;"[80] which, as already intimated, is not to be attained

73 Psalm 37:16.
74 Matthew 5:45.
75 Acts 11:24.
76 Matthew 12:35a.
77 Acts 24:15.
78 Psalm 1:5-6.
79 I Peter 4:18.
80 James 3:2.

in this life. And Paul says: "Let us lay aside every weight, and the sin (mark) which doth so easily beset us."[81] This the children of God do yet daily feel, more or less, which they must often with pain, shame, and sorrow, confess and lament, before God and man. And the farther they advance in Christianity, the more vile and depressed, they will ofttimes feel in themselves.

No willful sin!

Yet is this difference to be observed, that the converted do no longer, like the unconverted, knowingly and willingly, maliciously and designedly live in sin, but do earnestly hate, and seek to avoid it; and also daily strive and struggle against it, and feel like Paul to ask, "How shall we that are dead to sin, live any longer therein?" Rom. 6:2. Neither are "they any more the servants of sin." v. 22. God's children do not wish to sin any more, neither do they live in vicious sins. But nevertheless, are they frequently, out of weakness, overtaken unawares, to do that which they would not; for which they will earnestly pray for forgiveness, and do also lead a penitent life. And although they often painfully feel their great weakness, with which they are yet encompassed, they are nevertheless in Christ, as the branch is in the vine. And it is also, and will remain, an incontestable truth, that no man can at the same time, serve two opposite masters; that no man can, at the same time, walk on the broad and narrow way; that no man can, at the same time, hold with Christ and Belial; that no man can, at the same time, be in the light and in darkness; and that no one can, at the same time, be converted and unconverted; and that no one can, at the same time, be pious and ungodly, righteous and unrighteous, holy and unholy, a saint and a sinner, a child of God, and a child of the devil: "for he that is not with me, is against me (says Jesus), and he that gathereth not with me, scattereth abroad."[82] A person must be either in the fold of Christ or out of it. Depend upon it, here it will never do to "halt between two opinions."[83] Neither can any man be cold and hot at the same time. Therefore, O man, prove your own self, whether you are with or against Jesus.

81 Hebrews 12:1.
82 Matthew 12:30.
83 I Kings 18:21.

A personal call

Oh, I hope, dear reader, that you are not against Jesus, such a kind and lovely friend! O, how could you be opposed to Him who died for you out of love, to save you from sin and death, and to make you happy forever? Do pause and reflect seriously, before it is forever too late. O remember, you have a soul to be saved or lost forever. Also think of the great love of God toward poor, fallen mankind, and that he was so kind and willing, that all who would, might obtain mercy and find grace, and be saved from their sad condition; yea, that he even therefore sent his beloved Son into the world "to save sinners." Who also out of pure love gave himself willingly as a sacrifice, to accomplish that end, and offered his innocent life upon the cross, and shed his precious blood, which will cleanse true believers from all their sins. And after his resurrection, he also commanded "that repentance and forgiveness of sins should be preached in his name among all nations."

The offer still stands!

These glad tidings are still as valid as ever, and stand unaltered to this our day, in favor of contrite sinners, if they will avail themselves of them. God still commandeth all men everywhere to repent. Therefore all those who are truly sincere in seeking after salvation with all their heart and soul, need not at all to be discouraged, but may confidingly and cheerfully come to Jesus, who so willingly receives mourning and penitent sinners, to save them, and to make them eternally happy. Therefore, O ye poor sinners, do but heartily "repent and be converted" before it is forever too late, for "except ye repent, ye shall . . . perish."[84] And, "except ye be converted and become as little children, ye shall not enter into the kingdom of heaven."[85] Therefore delay no longer, in true faith to come to Jesus, the true friend of brokenhearted sinners, to be converted to him, and he will comfort you, "and ye shall find rest unto your souls,"[86] now in time, and in eternity. And besides, you can also thereby yet create a joy in heaven before the angels of God. O how encouraging and comforting to a contrite, penitent

84 Luke 13:3, 5.
85 Matthew 18:3.
86 Matthew 11:29.

soul, are the words, "I say unto you, that likewise joy shall be in heaven, over one sinner that repenteth, more than over ninety and nine just persons, which need no repentance."

Thus there is joy in heaven above
When sinners do repent:
O come then, sinners, great and small,
Now turn, your sins lament.
Create a joy in heav'n's domain
Before the angels there;
Where you shall with them equal be—
O what a graceful share!
Joy in the beauteous heavens there,
Before God's angel band—
O, how consoling is the word!—
There all who will may land,
Where will be joy in full supply;
There at God's own right hand;
How lovely and how beautiful
'Tis in the fatherland.
O joy! how great that joy will be!
Which ever will remain:
There is no grief no sorrow there,
Nor ever any pain.
O do but come, poor sinners now,
Ye who yet go astray,
To Jesus who yet calleth you
As Shepherd and the Way.
He will you in his kingdom lead,
Of joy and glory fair,
Where you shall be as Jesus is—
O come and do prepare;
And harden now your hearts no more.
Come, seek today God's face;
Your highest duty yet fulfill,
Now in the time of grace.

For more excellent titles and other material by the same author, call or write for a free catalog:

Sermon on the Mount Publishing
P.O. Box 246
Manchester, MI 48158
(734) 428-0488

the-witness@sbcglobal.net

www.kingdomreading.com